FINDING a CAREER

Careers If You Like Math

Barbara Sheen

ReferencePoint Press®

San Diego, CA

© 2017 ReferencePoint Press, Inc.
Printed in the United States

For more information, contact:
ReferencePoint Press, Inc.
PO Box 27779
San Diego, CA 92198
www. ReferencePointPress.com

LIBRARY OF CONGRESS CATALOGING-IN-PUBLICATION DATA

Name: Sheen, Barbara, author.
Title: Careers if you like math / by Barbara Sheen.
Description: San Diego, CA : ReferencePoint Press, Inc., [2017]. | Series: Finding a career | Audience: Grades 9 to 12. | Includes bibliographical references and index.
Identifiers: LCCN 2015045005 (print) | LCCN 2015049225 (ebook) | ISBN 9781682820049 (hardback) | ISBN 9781682820056 (epub)
Subjects: LCSH: Mathematics--Vocational guidance--Juvenile literature. | Mathematicians--Juvenile literature.
Classification: LCC QA10.5 .S54 2017 (print) | LCC QA10.5 (ebook) | DDC 510.23--dc23
LC record available at http://lccn.loc.gov/2015045005

CONTENTS

Introduction: Lots of Choices

If you like math and want to use it in your career, you're in luck. Employers need people with a strong math background. Mastering math not only gives you the ability to work with numbers but also teaches you to think logically, analyze and solve problems, identify patterns, and pay attention to detail. These skills are highly desirable. In fact, a 2015 survey conducted by the National Association of Colleges and Employers found that the ability to solve problems and analyze numerical data is among the top ten skills employers seek. So, bottom line: you're in demand.

Math Skills Are Useful in Every Industry

Indeed, your mathematical know-how can help you succeed in hundreds of occupations in every imaginable career field. As Steve Traylen, a math lover and systems administrator, explains in an interview in *Plus* magazine, "When you attack a math problem you have to work out precisely what the question is . . . think of all the consequences, and come out with the best solution. That skill is something you can apply in lots of areas."

Some occupations, such as an accountant, actuary, or mathematician, focus mainly on numbers. There are also lots of other occupations in which math-savvy individuals can combine their math skills with knowledge specific to their career field. In the world of big business, for example, professionals must know all about their product; they also must be able to work with budgets, use spreadsheets, calculate costs, measure profits, and solve problems. These are skills that come easily to math lovers, giving you an advantage over your less-mathematical peers. In addition, most companies gather huge amounts of data concerning different aspects of business. Businesses are scrambling to find detail-oriented people who can organize and analyze this data—mathematical people like you.

If you prefer working in health care, your math background is needed here, too. Physicians, for example, use math every day in their practice. They rely on arithmetic to calculate what dosage of medication to give patients based on the patient's weight. And they use their problem-solving skills combined with statistics and probability to determine the most effective treatment to prescribe. As Yale professor Ian Ayres explains in an article on the We Use Math website, "Evidence-based medicine, the use of statistical models to guide diagnoses and treatment, is already changing how doctors practice."

If building things is your passion, jobs in the construction industry need your skills, too. Measuring is a key element of a carpenter's job, and electricians use trigonometry to determine the correct angle for bending conduit (insulated tubing that wires are passed through). Likewise, architects and civil engineers couldn't design buildings without trigonometry and geometry. As David Farmer, a Florida civil engineer, explains in an article on the Mathematical Association of America website, "As a Civil Engineer a large part of my job consists of calculating and analyzing various situations. . . . Without my math foundation, I would not be competent to design roads, drainage systems, flood relief projects or water and sewer systems." In fact, mathematics is a fundamental tool in all engineering careers. Math is also used by professionals in computer and physical science. For instance, computer programmers use math to build complex applications, and astronomers rely on mathematical formulas to describe and determine planetary motion.

Since math is used in virtually every field, if you have a special area of interest, you can unite your love of math with your other passions. So, if you're wild about sports, you can pursue a career as a sports statistician. Artists can merge their artistic and mathematical talents in fields like computer graphics and video game design. So can fashionistas; believe it or not, math plays a key role in textile and fashion design. Measuring, repeating patterns in textile design, creating clothing patterns, and turning two-dimensional designs into three-dimensional garments all depend on math.

Opportunities, Compensation, and Satisfaction

As someone with super math skills, not only can you find work in virtually any career field, but you and your skills are quite special as well (of course, you already knew that). According to the US Center for Educational Statistics, one in five adults lacks the math skills expected of an eighth-grader. As a result, employers often find it difficult to find employees for math-related positions. A Millennial Branding survey found that nearly half of all employers surveyed reported that competition to hire individuals with a strong math background is high. In fact, it's not uncommon for individuals with math skills to receive multiple job offers.

And, since the demand for men and women like you often exceeds the supply of applicants, starting salaries for math-related jobs are quite good. A 2015 report conducted by Pay Scale, a career compensation database, ranked the average starting salaries for a variety of college majors. Mathematics, actuarial mathematics, and statistics were ranked among the top thirty highest-paying majors. Having strong math skills was also a common factor in most of the other top-paying majors, many of which were in engineering and computer science.

In addition to excellent pay, individuals in math-related careers report high levels of job satisfaction. When JobsRated.com ranked job satisfaction based on income, work environment, physical demands, and stress for two hundred different occupations, mathematician was the top-rated career, followed by actuary and statistician. Rob Hemmings, a British statistician who analyzes the effectiveness of new medications, comments in *Plus* magazine, "If I meet people and they ask what I do and I say 'medical statistician' it doesn't sound very interesting at all. . . . But if you actually explain what the job is . . . it makes it sound rather grand. I enjoy the fact that I can think I'm making a difference." And, with your math skills, so can you.

Actuary

A Few Facts

Number of Jobs
As of 2014, about 21,490

Salaries
As of 2014, the mean annual salary was $110,090

Educational Requirements
Minimum of a bachelor's degree

Personal Qualities
Good communication skills; detail oriented; analytical; likes working with numbers

Work Settings
Indoors in an office

Future Job Outlook
Job growth of 27 percent by 2020, which is much faster than average

What the Heck Is an Actuary?

Everyone knows that teens pay way more for car insurance than adults. The question is, why? The answer: because an actuary determined that teens are more likely to make insurance claims than adults, which raises the insurer's financial risk, which leads to higher rates, which shield the insurance company from losing money when teen drivers file claims. Simple, right? Okay, not so simple.

It took an actuary—or, more likely, quite a few actuaries—hours to work out this scenario. They didn't just pull it off the top of their heads. They worked it out with numbers and with probabilities. By combing through large statistical databases and using mathematical formulas to analyze their findings, actuaries predict the probability of an individual or group experiencing a major life-changing event, such as retirement, death, sickness, or property loss. They use math, statistics, and probability to calculate what the occurrence of such events will cost insurance companies and pension funds in terms of insurance claims and retirement benefits. Then they come up with financial solutions aimed at protecting these organizations from having to pay out more money than they take in. As an article on Be an Actuary.org explains, "Insurance companies, financial planners, and many multinational corporations are hesitant to make certain moves without consulting us first. That's because the problems we solve provide a safeguard against catastrophe and this gives them the confidence to grow."

A Typical Workday

Describing the typical workday for an actuary isn't easy, mainly because there is no typical workday. In this job, every day is different depending on the type of project an actuary is tackling. Different types of actuaries work on different projects.

Actuaries can be generalists, who deal with all kinds of projects, or they can specialize in a particular area. Casualty actuaries, for example, focus on property and liability insurance. Life actuaries concentrate on life and health insurance, and employee benefits or pension actuaries help manage the risk involved in pension plans. Yet no matter the specialty, actuaries spend a lot of time seated in front of computers gathering facts and figures from large databases. Using mathematical and problem-solving skills, they analyze this data in order to come up with predictions about financial risk as well as proposals on how to lessen that risk. Actuaries use specialized software to create tables, charts, reports, and spreadsheets to illustrate their findings. As British actuary Kathy Byrnes explains in an interview in *Plus* magazine, "Actuarial work is more about interpreting the mathematical results you get and making commercial decisions based on those results. It's about combining math with commercial realities and using it practically in applications."

When actuaries aren't poring over facts and figures, they're attending meetings. Actuaries usually work in teams. Team members meet often to discuss the projects they are working on. Actuaries also meet with clients, executives, managers, and other professionals. At these meetings, they present the charts, tables, and reports they've prepared. Since not everyone involved may have a math background, actuaries are responsible for explaining their findings in a way everyone can understand.

In addition to these tasks, actuaries may be asked to speak before public agencies about proposed laws concerning insurance rates. Likewise, they may be called on to serve as expert witnesses in court cases, providing actuarial evidence on the long-term cost to victims of crimes, car accidents, and injuries. In an interview in *Plus* magazine, Irish actuary Shane Whelan describes this part of his job: "This work involved sitting down with the case papers, ascertaining the loss, working through the tax calculations, and then capitalizing that loss for the rest of their lives. It was very hands-on."

A Top-Rated Profession

"The actuarial career is great for anyone that enjoys analytical problem solving and developing creative business solutions. It is consistently rated as a top profession, and it provides a variety of interesting work, great job security and competitive compensation."

Lauren Ford, quoted in "A Day in the Life of an Actuary," Investopedia, September 5, 2013. www.investopedia.com.

Educational Requirements

Actuaries must have a minimum of a bachelor's degree. Most actuaries major in mathematics, statistics, or actuarial science. The coursework is challenging: classes in linear algebra, advanced calculus, statistics, probability, and numerical analysis are the norm. Likewise, computer science classes prepare actuaries to work with databases, spreadsheets, and specialized software.

Taking advanced math courses in high school can help prepare students for a career as an actuary. And, because actuaries must be able to speak and write well, and must understand economics to make accurate predictions, classes in English, speech, business, and economics are also helpful.

What About Exams?

Test taking is a way of life for an actuary. Over the course of their careers, actuaries are required to successfully complete a series of ten exams. Since the first two exams assess knowledge of college-level math and most employers prefer new hires to have successfully completed these two exams before coming on board, most actuarial candidates take these preliminary exams before they graduate. As John Parkinson, a Philadelphia actuary, explained in a 2015 interview on the Society for Industrial and Applied Mathematics website, "Undergraduates should investigate an actuarial career and the corresponding professional exams as early as possible. Getting a head start on actuarial exams is a big career plus."

Once on the job, the exams continue. These tests are tough. It's not uncommon for experienced actuaries to have to take an exam more than once in order to get a passing grade. Many employers help candidates by providing them with on-the-job study sessions. And, in order to reward the time and effort it takes to successfully complete each exam, some firms will give you a bonus for each test you complete successfully. Life, health, and pension actuaries who successfully complete five of the ten exams receive associate certification by the Society of Actuaries. The Casualty Actuarial Society grants property and liability actuaries associate certification when they pass seven out of the ten exams. Associates are given greater responsibility and higher wages. An actuary who passes all ten exams earns a fellow certification, which is the highest actuarial rank. Holding this rank is extremely prestigious, and fellows are compensated accordingly.

Preparing for Actuary Jobs

The best way to get a foot in the door, so to speak, is to get an internship. A college-level internship with an insurance company or an actuarial consulting firm is a great way to get practical experience—and make connections with people in the industry. Interns get on-the-job training as well as a chance to apply what they've learned in college to real actuarial work. They're mentored by an actuarial associate and have opportunities to network with other interns, experienced actuaries, and senior management. Many actuarial internship positions are paid, and some firms will give interns a housing and transportation allowance. And, if interns do well, there's an excellent chance that they'll be offered employment upon graduation. To sweeten the deal, some firms offer new hires a signing bonus and tuition reimbursement, too. College counselors can help you find an appropriate internship position. In addition, many companies post actuarial internship positions on the Internet.

Skills and Character Traits

Actuarial work isn't for everyone. Sometimes actuaries work alone; sometimes they work in a team—and they have to be comfortable with both. And just having awesome math skills isn't enough. Actuaries have to like the idea of spending a good part of each day working with numbers. Because actuaries analyze a variety of documents and data, their analytical skills must be sharp. In addition, actuaries should have good oral and written communication skills so they can present reports clearly and effectively. On Risk Is Opportunity, a website that promotes actuarial careers, Indiana actuary Timothy Bischof states that "communication is key. Those who can summarize and synthesize what they did . . . will rise to the top. Those who can't, won't."

Working Conditions and Salaries

Most actuaries are employed by insurance companies or actuarial consulting firms. The latter are companies that handle actuarial services for organizations that don't have in-house actuaries. Actuaries work a traditional forty-hour workweek in a comfortable office environment. They rarely have to work overtime. So, if you want a job that doesn't dominate the rest of your life, this is it. In fact, the 2015 *Jobs Rated Almanac* ranks a career as an actuary as a low-stress career.

Low stress, however, doesn't mean low pay. Actuaries are well compensated. Out of three hundred possible occupations, the career-planning website MyPlan.com named actuary the forty-first best-paying career in the United States. What an actuary earns

A Day in the Life of an Actuary

"I manage the rates we charge in a handful of states. Daily, things change depending on where we are in the rate review process. My team manages the rates, provides analysis of where things currently stand, and handles the state filing requirements. What I like most is that the analysis itself is extremely statistical in nature, but when it comes to what is implemented we not only have to consider the statistical side but also the real world application and the potential impact from a business perspective."

Kelly Hernandez, "What Is Working as an Actuary Really Like?," Be An Actuary, 2015. www.beanactuary.org.

depends on his or her experience, credentials, and geographic location. According to the Bureau of Labor Statistics (BLS), typical salaries range from about $58,080 to $180,680, although actuarial fellows with more than twenty years of experience have the potential to earn much more. The BLS also reports that, as of 2014, the mean annual salary for all actuaries was $110,090. In addition, actuaries receive generous employee benefits, including health insurance, retirement benefits, and paid vacation and sick days. And, as actuaries pass their exams, they can advance to supervisory positions overseeing other actuaries and actuarial teams.

What's the Future Outlook for Actuaries?

This is a hot career field. Currently, about 24,300 actuaries work in the United States. The BLS predicts that jobs for actuaries will increase by 26 percent through 2022, which is more than double the average for all occupations. So, if you think you want to be an actuary, there's a good chance employers will be clamoring to hire you. And, odds are you'll like what you do. Numerous surveys of actuaries found that this career consistently ranks high in job satisfaction.

Indeed, out of two hundred occupations, CareerCast.com ranked actuary number one in job satisfaction. As Tonya Manning, a North Carolina actuary, comments in an article on the CareerCast website, "I've never met an actuary who said they didn't love what they do. I work with interesting people every day, from CFOs [chief financial officers] and attorneys to international clients. . . . And since I love solving problems that benefit society, it's really a wonderful career."

Find Out More

Be an Actuary.org
website: www.beanactuary.org

This website, sponsored by the Casualty Actuary Society and the Society of Actuaries, offers a wealth of information about the career, including information about what actuaries do, salaries, college programs, and internships.

Casualty Actuarial Society (CAS)
website: www.casact.org

The CAS is a professional organization of casualty actuaries. It provides information about actuarial exams, journals, job postings, and sponsors scholarships.

Risk Is Opportunity
website: www.riskisopportunity.net

This website is dedicated to promoting actuarial careers. It provides interviews with actuaries who discuss a typical workday, videos offering advice about internships and exams, facts about the career, and university visits.

Society of Actuaries (SOA)
website: www.soa.org

The SOA is the largest professional actuary organization in the world. It provides a wealth of information about the career, exams, and actuarial issues. It also provides links to other informative actuarial websites.

Atmospheric Scientist

A Few Facts

Number of Jobs
As of 2014, about 10,850

Salaries
As of 2014, the mean annual salary was $88,090

Educational Requirements
Minimum of a bachelor's degree

Personal Qualities
Good critical-thinking and computer skills; adaptable; likes working outdoors

Work Settings
Indoors and outdoors

Future Job Outlook
Job growth of 10 percent through 2022, which is about as fast as average

It's All About the Weather

"Everyone talks about the weather, but no one does anything about it," an old saying goes. When it comes to atmospheric scientists, that saying isn't entirely correct. Atmospheric scientists are weather experts. They study short-term weather systems in order to predict the weather and its impact. They also research long-term climate conditions in an effort to predict future climate events, such as global warming, drought, and ozone depletion. They use mathematical instruments like thermometers and barometers to collect data and algebra to figure out how different variables like wind speed or humidity might affect the weather. The information they collect and analyze does more than help people decide whether to take an umbrella—it saves lives by warning the public about dangerous weather events so that they can prepare for what's coming. It also alerts the world to dangerous long-term climatic changes. If you find weather intriguing but you want to do more than just *talk* about it, an atmospheric scientist career might be worth considering.

Are All Atmospheric Scientists the Same?

There are a number of different types of atmospheric scientists, making this a field that offers lots of career options. Meteorologists are probably the most well-known type of atmospheric scientist. Meteorologists study short-term weather systems. But exactly what they do depends on the type of meteorologist they are. There are several kinds.

Operational meteorologists are the largest group. They collect data related to air pressure, wind velocity, humidity, and temperature from satellites, radar, and nearly ten thousand weather stations located all over the world. Using statistics, mathematical calculations, and sophisticated computer software, they analyze this data in order to predict the weather.

Research meteorologists are another group. As the name implies, they do research related to climate and weather. For example, in an effort to make air travel safer, British research meteorologist Helen Hewson is studying airflow over mountains. In an interview in *Plus* magazine, she comments on her job: "The aim is to tell aircraft pilots if it's windy in a particular way over specific mountains then you may get effects which are dangerous and you have to avoid them, but if it's windy in another way then you should be able to fly over them." Research meteorologists also develop new data-collecting instruments and weather-prediction software.

Broadcast meteorologists are still another group. Also known as weather forecasters, they report the weather on television, radio, and the Internet. In making their forecasts, they depend on data gathered by operational meteorologists as well as local weather maps and charts. On the air, they use specialized graphic software to illustrate their forecast. In many cases, they write the scripts for their reports. In an interview on the Job Shadow website, Matt Meister, chief meteorologist at station KRDO in Colorado Springs, Colorado, explains, "I make and present the forecast for our website, mobile apps, news radio station and 5, 6 and 10pm newscasts [Monday through Friday]. Additionally I supervise the other members of Stormtracker13 . . . and I oversee the maintenance of our 20+ weather computers. . . . In simplest terms my job consists of two things: 1) making the forecast and 2) giving it out!"

Studying and forecasting short-term weather events appeals to some atmospheric scientists—but not all. Those who prefer to focus on long-term global climate conditions are called climatologists. Climatologists study past weather patterns in order to forecast shifts in climate that are likely to occur in the future. For instance, in an effort to predict global warming trends, climatologists have been taking samples from different levels of Antarctica's ice core. By analyzing the thickness of the ice samples at various levels, and the amount of carbon dioxide (which rises as temperatures rise) trapped in the samples, they can determine what the climate was like at different points in time. This gives them a long-term view of changes in climate. Climatologists use this information to develop three-dimensional global climate models, which illustrate past climate events and how even the smallest changes in climate affect the ice core. These findings make it possible for them to make predictions related to future climate change, such as how much longer the ice core can continue to exist under the current rate of global warming.

What Does Math Have to Do with Atmospheric Science?

Although atmospheric science sounds interesting, you might be wondering what in the world this career field has to do with math. The answer is, plenty. Even though math is not the primary focus of atmospheric science, a strong math background is important to the job. Atmospheric scientists use calculus, geometry, and algebra in predicting the weather and climate trends. And they rely on their skills in graphing, data collecting, recognizing patterns, and problem solving. To forecast weather, for example, meteorologists collect numerical data concerning wind speed and direction, temperature, humidity, and air pressure from weather balloons, satellites, and radar. They plot this data on graphs, charts, and weather maps, which they analyze looking for patterns related to weather trends. Mathematics figures prominently in their analysis. They also use computer software to solve complex equations that help them understand the relationship between different atmospheric factors and how changes in any of these variables affect the weather. According to Barry Lough, the creator of Stuff in the Air, a meteorology website, "The mathematics used in meteorology could, and does, fill textbooks quite extensively."

Preparing for This Career

If you decide to become an atmospheric scientist, you'll need a minimum of a bachelor's degree. Research meteorologists need a master's or doctorate degree. In college, the best choice of a major will be atmospheric science or a related field like geology. Atmospheric science classes cover subjects like meteorology and climatology and include hands-on classes in the use of forecasting instruments. In addition, you'll take courses in computer science, statistics, calculus, and other advanced mathematics. In fact, math is so important in this field that successful completion of four years of high school math is often a prerequisite for this major. In addition, if your goal is to become a broadcast meteorologist, you'll take classes in speech, journalism, and broadcasting.

If your goal is broadcast meteorology, you should get all of the public speaking and broadcasting experience you can to build your confidence and speaking skills. This may include working at a school radio or television station or a community-access television station. For instance, while still a

A Passion for Weather

"I've had a passion for atmospheric science since about the age of 8 when I first realized a winter storm forming in the foothills of the Colorado Rockies often meant a snow day off from school in Montreal 3 days later. Watching with awe as summer lightning and hail storms formed overhead further solidified this passion in Earth and atmospheric sciences."

Bill Coulter, quoted in "Exclusive: Q & A with CP24 Breakfast Meteorologist—Bill Coulter," MediaCareers.ca, August 29, 2012. www.mediacareers.ca.

young teenager, Matt DiPirro, a meteorologist at KSWO in Lawton, Oklahoma, gained his first on-air experience by reporting live during snowstorms for his local community-access television station. He continued honing his broadcasting skills by working at his college television station. He says that these experiences helped assure him that he'd chosen the right career path and gave him the confidence he needed to succeed as a broadcast meteorologist.

A summer internship working on a research project involving weather is another great way to gain hands-on experience in atmospheric science and network with people already working in the field. Organizations like the National Weather Service, Significant Opportunities in Atmospheric Research and Science, and Young Leaders in Climate Change (YLCC) all offer such programs. For example, in 2015 YLCC interns stationed in national parks studied how issues related to climate change impacted the parks. Colleges can help their students find this program and others. Many of these programs offer paid internships along with free or subsidized housing and a travel stipend.

Making a Difference in People's Lives

"I have wanted to be a Meteorologist since I was 9. There's a saying 'If you love what you do, you never work a day in your life.' That certainly holds true for me! This is my hobby that fortunately I get paid for! But . . . it's not about the dollar, it's about doing your job right, doing it accurately, and making sure you tell the people what they NEED to know. Your forecast makes a difference in people's lives, at times it even may save lives! . . . And man do I love it!"

Kevin Arnone, quoted in "Interview with Meteorologist Kevin Arnone." WXedge.com, January 31, 2015. http://wxedge.com.

A climatologist monitors solar activity at a North Pole research station. Climatologists use this type of information to develop models that help scientists study climate change.

Skills and Adaptability

You can't be an atmospheric scientist and *not* like science, math, computers, weather, and climate-related issues. But there's much more to this job. To succeed as an atmospheric scientist, you need to have strong critical-thinking skills, and you need to be a problem solver. Atmospheric scientists use these skills to analyze weather data, taking into account variables such as geographic factors that affect local weather conditions and past weather history in order to make accurate forecasts. And because they spend a lot of time in front of a computer screen analyzing data from satellites and other high-tech equipment, atmospheric scientists need to have computer smarts as well as the ability to work slowly and steadily through a lot of information.

Adaptability is another essential trait for an atmospheric scientist. Many work in ordinary office settings, but others work in remote weather stations with extremely challenging conditions. Broadcast meteorologists, for example, spend most of their time in a comfortable broadcasting studio. Yet they also broadcast from outdoor locations during major weather events. Many operational meteorologists work in weather stations located in isolated areas throughout the world. They spend a lot of time out in the field collecting weather data and are exposed to extreme weather conditions. Climatologists and research meteorologists work indoors in laboratories and offices as well as out in the field in places like Antarctica, where winter temperatures can fall to as low as -128°F (-89°C).

As an atmospheric scientist, you'll probably be employed by a private business or a college or university. About 29 percent work for the government. In most cases, atmospheric scientists work full-time, but their work schedules may not be traditional. In order to monitor the weather twenty-four hours a day, seven days a week, operational meteorologists usually work eight-hour shifts (sometimes at night); they also work on holidays and weekends. In addition, during severe weather events, broadcast and operational meteorologists have to work extended hours.

Earnings and Advancement Opportunities

According to the Bureau of Labor Statistics (BLS), as of 2014 the lowest 10 percent of atmospheric scientists earned less than $50,030, and the top 10 percent earned more than $128,670. It reported the mean annual salary was $88,090. In addition to the base salary, most atmospheric scientists receive employee benefits such as health insurance, travel stipends, retirement benefits, and paid vacation and sick days.

As atmospheric scientists gain experience, their salaries increase. As far as advancement goes, many atmospheric scientists advance to supervisory positions in which they oversee other atmospheric scientists. Broadcast meteorologists advance by moving to larger broadcasting markets.

What's the Future Job Outlook for Atmospheric Scientists?

Employment for atmospheric scientists is expected to grow by 10 percent through 2022, according to the BLS. This is about as fast as average for all occupations. However, this is a competitive career field. The BLS reports that the number of future meteorology graduates is expected to exceed the number of job openings. Getting a master's degree is one way to gain an edge over other candidates.

Despite the competition, once you're on the job, there's a good chance you'll like what you do. As Connecticut meteorologist Sam Kantrow said in a 2014 interview on WXEdge.com, "Every day is different, every day has challenges, but the rewards are incredible!"

Find Out More

American Meteorological Society (AMS)
www2.ametsoc.org

The AMS is a scientific and professional organization promoting and providing information about atmospheric science. Members include atmospheric scientists and students. It offers education and career-building information as well as college meteorology clubs.

Cornell Meteorology
http://ccams.eas.cornell.edu

The website of Cornell University's Meteorology Department offers advice and a list (with links) of various research opportunities for students seeking internships.

National Weather Association (NWA)
www.nwas.org

The NWA is a professional association of operational meteorologists. It offers information about careers in meteorology and sponsors scholarships.

National Weather Service
www.weather.gov

The National Weather Service is a governmental agency that provides data, forecasts, and warnings related to weather, water, and climate. It offers a wealth of information about the weather, careers in weather, and volunteer opportunities for young people.

Construction Design

What Is Construction Design?

When you were in kindergarten, did you knock the other children down in your rush to get to the building blocks? Were Legos your go-to toy? Was your favorite part of going to the beach building sand castles? If building things has always been one of your passions, you should consider a career in construction design.

Before any structure can be built, it must be carefully designed so that it is safe, environmentally sound, economical, functional, and aesthetically pleasing. Coming up with these designs is the job of construction design professionals. There are a number of different occupations related to construction design, including architects, civil engineers, urban planners, and landscape architects. Of these, architects and civil engineers are among the largest groups. Architects design buildings. They're the masterminds behind the look and functionality of houses, apartments, hospitals, schools, banks, and soaring skyscrapers, among other structures. Civil engineers focus on larger construction projects like roads, bridges, and dams. They also design transportation facilities like airports

and ports and infrastructure such as water, energy, and waste systems.

These professionals combine art, math, computer science, and physics to do their job. If you like art, problem solving, and mathematics; have a good understanding of space and dimensions; and want to leave a tangible mark on the world, you might want to explore a career in architecture or civil engineering. As St. Louis architect Darlene Rutkowski-Hanks explains in an interview on the National Council of Architectural Registration Boards website, "I love being able to take a concept, place it on paper, see it physically built, and then watch people enjoying it."

A Typical Workday

Both architects and civil engineers have many responsibilities. In both jobs, their work begins before they start the design process. One of the first things they do is meet with clients to discuss the proposed project. Once they have all of the details, they conduct a study to determine whether the project is viable. For architects, this involves researching local zoning laws, fire regulations, and environmental issues that may affect the project. For civil engineers, the study involves running soil and underground tests on the site to see whether the ground can safely support the proposed structure.

Architects and civil engineers also review survey maps of the site and data concerning construction and labor costs. Once this work is completed, they begin designing the structure. They may do the first draft by hand, but they use computer-aided design and drafting software to produce the final plans, which include a set of three-dimensional blueprints drawn to scale showing the exact dimensions of every part of the structure. They also prepare a written report that describes the specific types and quantity of building materials to be used on the structure and their costs. Likewise, they're involved in setting up a project budget and a construction schedule. Their involvement in the project doesn't end with the design. They visit the building site often to monitor the construction process. When problems occur, they're the ones who solve them. They also frequently touch base with their clients to make sure clients are happy with the outcome. Civil engineers are also responsible for inspecting, maintaining, and repairing the structure on a preset schedule for years to come.

Where Does Math Fit In?

In construction design, math is everywhere. All building design is based on geometry. Architects and civil engineers use it to calculate the size, shape, and volume of all the components of a structure. In addition, they use algebra and physics to determine the effect of various forces, like strong winds, on the structure and the best way to counteract negative effects. As architect Lee Calisti noted in a January 2015 article on the Life of an Architect website, "One needs to be adept at math, namely algebra, geometry and trigonometry, to deal with the array of dimensions, quantities, area, volume and other geometric relationships. This plays into spatial thinking and patterns."

Architects and civil engineers also depend on math to measure and perform simple calculations. In addition, it helps them make business decisions. They use math to calculate the quantities and cost of materials, equipment, and labor and to set up budgets and construction schedules.

What About College?

Architects and civil engineers must graduate from college. Civil engineers are required to have a minimum of a bachelor of science degree from a college or university accredited by the Accreditation Board for Engineering and Technology. It typically takes four years to earn this degree. Architects are required to have a minimum of a bachelor of architecture degree from an architectural program accredited by the National Architectural Accrediting Board. Accredited architectural programs typically take five years to complete.

College coursework for both of these careers is challenging and, lucky for you, includes higher-level math courses like linear algebra and calculus along with classes in physics, art and design, and computer science. Architecture and civil engineering students also take required liberal arts classes as well as courses specific to either profession. The latter are usually combined with labs in which students get to experiment with different materials and designs. As Taha Marhaba, chairman of the Department of Civil and Environmental Engineering at the New Jersey Institute of Technology, explains on the school's website, "Students are always working on projects in the labs, which makes their work interesting and ever-developing. . . . In our construction materials lab, students work with the materials used in civil engineering such as concrete and steel."

In high school you should take physics, advanced math, computer science, and art classes, which will help you succeed later in college. Classes in language arts and speech will also help you since communication skills are essential in both of these occupations.

What About Licensing?

Both architects and civil engineers must be licensed. Requirements vary by state. Typically, once architecture students have their degree, they do a three-year paid architectural internship. This involves working under the supervision of a licensed architect. To receive a license, architects must successfully complete the Architect Registration Exam.

Civil engineers follow a similar path. Upon receiving a bachelor's degree, candidates must successfully complete the Fundamentals of Engineering Exam. Passing the exam earns candidates the title of a civil engineering intern or an engineer-in-training (EIT). With four years of work experience and successful completion of a second exam, EITs are granted a professional engineer's license. Only professional engineers can legally head up construction projects. In an interview on PBS.org, Patricia Frayre, an EIT, talks about the process:

> When you graduate college, you take an eight-hour exam, and if you pass it, then you become an EIT. You then have to work for four years with a registered, professional

engineer after which you become eligible to take another exam to get your professional engineer's license. . . . If you pass it, then you become a registered, professional engineer. That's the next milestone in my career. Right now, I'm working on my experience. Once I become a professional engineer, there's really no stopping me.

Exploring Construction Design

If you want to learn more about either profession before making a career choice, you should consider job shadowing an architect or civil engineer for at least a day. Another way to learn about the construction process is by working on a construction project as part of a road or construction crew. This might be a part-time or summer job, or you can volunteer with a group like Habitat for Humanity. You can also join a civil engineering or architecture club. Both the American Society of Civil Engineers and the American Institute of Architecture Students sponsor clubs for high school and college students throughout the United States. Members of both groups are able to attend workshops, meet construction design professionals, and participate in hands-on construction service projects.

Skills and Work Environment

Construction design requires a broad set of skills. Architects and civil engineers need to know a lot about design and construction methods, tools, and materials. They also must understand engineering principles and physics and have a strong math background. They should be creative, good problem solvers, and decisive. And, since the smallest error in design can lead to a potential disaster, they must be extremely detail oriented. Construction designers also should have good interpersonal and communication skills since they must interact with clients and construction professionals.

Math Is the Key to Engineering

"Math and physics are really the keys to engineering, especially engineering structures, because physics tells you how structures behave when you push against them, when you pull against them, and how they will react in the wind and under earthquakes and under the load of occupants. Mathematics is the tool that you use to calculate the physical effects. So you use both mathematics and the physical sciences."

Matthys Levy, quoted in "Who Builds Big Interview." PBS. www.pbs.org.

As a construction designer you'll work both in an office and out in the field. Plus, if you like to travel, you're in luck because many civil engineering firms are involved in large global projects. Civil engineers may have to travel or live abroad while working on a particular project.

No matter where a project is located, construction designers will usually work a traditional forty-hour week. However, they may put in more hours to meet construction deadlines. Most construction designers are employed by architectural or engineering firms; others work for government agencies. Some architects and civil engineers are self-employed.

What About Compensation and Advancement?

According to the Bureau of Labor Statistics (BLS), as of 2014 most architects earned between $44,940 and $121,910; salaries for civil engineers ranged from about $52,570 to $128,110. Since architects and civil engineers must be licensed to work unsupervised, their salaries will be at the lower end of the pay scale until they are licensed. With the exception of self-employed individuals, most architects and civil engineers also receive employee benefits such as health insurance, retirement benefits, and paid vacation and sick days. Plus, if you like the idea of being self-employed, after many years of experience you can open your own design firm.

A Bright Future

The BLS predicts that employment opportunities for civil engineers will grow by about 20 percent and for architects about 17 percent by 2022. So, if this is a career path that interests you, your future looks bright.

Find Out More

American Architectural Foundation (AAF)
website: www.archfoundation.org

The AAF is an association of architects and other individuals interested in the environmental future of cities. It offers information on careers in architecture and architecture scholarships.

American Institute of Architecture Students (AIAS)
website: http://aias.org

The AIAS provides information about accredited architectural college programs and matches students with professional mentors.

American Society for Engineering Education (ASEE)
website: www.asee.org

The ASEE promotes engineering education. It offers a variety of publications dealing with careers in engineering and information about scholarships.

American Society of Civil Engineers (ASCE)
website: www.asce.org

The ASCE sponsors student clubs and provides information about civil engineering careers, licenses, scholarships, and civil engineering degree programs.

Educator

A Source of Inspiration

If you love math, chances are an educator helped spark your passion. If you want to do the same for the next generation, pursuing a career as a math educator may be just what you're looking for. This is exactly what high school math teacher Leila Torrez did. In an interview in the fall/winter 2015–2016 edition of *Las Cruces Magazine*, Torrez explained, "I wanted to be the kind of teacher who made math both understandable and enjoyable for my students."

Math at Every Level

As a math educator, you can work with any age level you prefer. For instance, if you love being around young children, you can become an elementary school teacher. As an elementary school teacher, you may teach the same group of students throughout the day in all academic subjects, including math, or you may be responsible for teaching only math to students in a particular grade level. On the Teacher Certification Degrees website,

South Carolina fifth-grade math teacher Bridget Pearsall comments, "I teach math to three classes of 30 students. The team of fifth-grade teachers I work with have collaborated to divide the students up into their three classes based on the type of learner they are, and at what pace they seem to work best."

If you prefer working with teenagers, you can teach math in middle or high school. On this level, each math teacher is responsible for teaching various math courses to one or more grade levels. For instance, a high school math teacher may teach introductory algebra to ninth-graders, advanced algebra to tenth-graders, and geometry to eleventh-graders.

If instructing older teens and adults is more your speed, you can teach mathematics in a college or university. In this capacity, educators provide instruction in one particular field of math, such as statistics, or teach a variety of math courses. You can also instruct adults as a math curriculum developer or specialist. These math educators act as a math resource person for elementary and secondary teachers. They are typically experienced math teachers who have advanced to a specialist position.

What Does the Job Entail?

Since you've been going to school for what might seem like forever, you may think you know exactly what math educators do.

But the truth is that educators do more than meets the eye. For example, in addition to providing subject matter instruction, kindergarten through twelfth-grade (K-12) teachers help students develop study skills, thinking skills, and test-taking skills. Their job also involves lots of paperwork, including preparing lesson plans and grading student work, as well as performing duties like monitoring the hallways. Sponsoring student organizations, providing tutoring sessions, conferencing with parents, and attending meetings and professional development sessions are also parts of their jobs.

Professional development sessions are often conducted by math curriculum specialists. They assist teachers in improving their skills, and they design and develop math curriculum, instructional strategies, and assessment activities for school districts.

Postsecondary math educators wear many hats, too. As teachers, they may give lectures to several hundreds of students at a time, instruct smaller classes, and conduct seminars. They also grade papers, attend department meetings, and act as student advisers. In addition, some postsecondary educators conduct original research in mathematics and write papers for publication describing the results of their research. Katie Evans, an assistant professor at Louisiana Tech University, describes her job in an interview on the Mathematical Association of America website: "Besides teaching undergraduate and graduate mathematics courses . . . I spend a significant amount of time . . . conducting research activities . . . and writing research results for journal publication. My position offers a balance of teaching and research activities."

How Do You Become a Math Educator?

If your goal is to be a K-12 math teacher, you'll need a minimum of a bachelor's degree from an accredited teacher education program. Depending on your state's teacher licensing requirements, you'll either major in education with a math minor or math with a minor in education. During these education classes, prospective educators visit different classrooms and observe teachers in action. They also are required to do a semester of student teaching under the guidance of an experienced teacher. In addition, they must successfully complete a licensing exam. In most states, an elementary license enables educators to teach kindergarten through eighth grade; a secondary license enables them to teach seventh through twelfth grade.

Other positions require advanced degrees. If you want to become a math curriculum specialist or a teacher in a two-year college, you'll need a minimum of a master's degree in mathematics. Math specialists are also required to have previous teaching experience and a teacher's license. Teaching in a four-year college usually requires a doctorate degree. This involves successfully completing two to six years of rigorous study beyond a master's degree, the writing of a book-length dissertation based on research conducted; and passing a qualifying exam that tests mathematics knowledge. No special license is required.

Is Teaching for You?

If you plan to teach math, you obviously need to be good at math. But just being good at something doesn't make you a teacher. It's the teaching part of the job that requires certain characteristics, talents, and skills. Think about your favorite math teachers. They're probably really good at explaining concepts. Clarity and overall communication skills are a big deal for math teachers. Creativity isn't a bad characteristic to have either. Keeping students engaged, especially students who might not like math as much as you do, can be challenging. Some educators try to introduce a little fun into their math lessons, but they never lose sight of the real objective. As Scott Keltner, a Kansas high school math teacher, relates in an interview on the Teacher Certification Degrees website, "'Have fun, while getting stuff done' is the mantra that governs my classes. . . . When students are able to do something—create an experience that engrains a concept in their mind—they more fully understand the topic and how it relates to a real-world application."

To be an educator, you should also like working with young people. And, since students come from diverse backgrounds, teachers must be respectful of cultural differences. In addition, they need to be patient, even-tempered, and thick-skinned. As you know from your own school experience, some students (not you, of course) act out; teachers must be able to handle difficult students without getting angry or taking improper behavior personally. Finally, if your ambition is to work in a university as a math educator, make sure you like the idea of doing research—not just teaching.

A good way to learn more about this career path is by volunteering to be a math tutor in an after-school program. Working in a summer camp is another experience that lets candidates test whether they enjoy instructing others. Likewise, joining a club like Future Teachers of America, which is dedicated to helping high school students explore teaching, is another great way to gain hands-on teaching experience. Club members get to try out their teaching skills by going into classrooms, where they help teachers and work with students. In most cases they earn service hours for their efforts, which reflect positively on college applications.

Making an Impact

"What I loved best about being a teacher was . . . knowing the impact that I made on that child whether it was academically in the classroom or outside in the real world. I loved the challenge of reaching out to them and teaching them math and seeing them excel in a subject that typically is not their favorite nor easiest one in school. The simple rewards of seeing their eyes light up or the raw emotion on their face when they have those 'aha' moments in mathematics and it all clicks for them."

Marc Dembowski, "Why I Chose to Teach," New Teacher Center, May 7, 2013. www.newteachercenter.org.

Working Conditions Vary

Most K-12 math educators and curriculum specialists are employed by public school districts or by private and parochial schools. Most postsecondary math educators are employed by public and private colleges and universities. Working conditions vary depending on the particular educational setting. Math curriculum specialists, for example, usually have an office in the school district's headquarters. However, they visit schools frequently and spend part of most workdays in transit. College professors, too, usually have their own office. K-12 teachers, on the other hand, usually don't have an office space. Instead, they have an assigned classroom within the school. Although most schools are pleasant and cheerful, some are overcrowded and in poor condition.

Math educators' work schedules also vary considerably. K-12 teachers' hours are set by the local school district. Most are on duty from 8 a.m. to 3 p.m., 185 to 190 days per year, with a paid two-month summer break and a one- to two-week winter and spring break. Postsecondary educators' schedules vary, too. Beyond scheduled classes and office hours, a professor's work schedule is usually flexible. Most work Monday through Friday, nine months per year, with a three-month summer break (during which many university professors continue to do research) and a one- to two-week winter and spring break. Unlike K-12 and postsecondary teachers, math curriculum developers usually work year-round. Typically, they have two to four weeks of vacation in the summer.

Earning and Advancement Opportunities

Salaries for math educators differ. Generally, salaries for all K-12 teachers are set by the school district and follow the same pay schedule no matter the level or subject. The Bureau of Labor Statistics (BLS) reports that as of 2014, salaries for K-12 teachers ranged from about $36,040 to about $88,910, with a mean annual salary of $59,330 for high school teachers, $57,620 for middle school teachers, and $56,830 for elementary school teachers. It reported that salaries for curriculum developers ranged from about $35,700 to about $95,590, with a mean annual salary of $64,040.

Earnings for postsecondary math educators depend on the level of education and years of experience. There are four types of full-time college and university teachers: instructors, assistant professors, associate professors, and full professors. Full professors are the highest ranking and the highest paid, followed by associate professors, assistant professors, and instructors. The American Association of University Professors reports that common salaries for college professors range from about $64,759 to $218,033, with an average yearly salary of $85,399.

Most math educators receive employee benefits that include health insurance, retirement benefits, and paid vacation and sick days. With experience and advanced degrees, math educators can advance to administrative positions.

How Does the Future Look?

If becoming a math educator interests you, you'll be welcomed into the field. The BLS predicts that by 2022 employment for elementary and middle school teachers will grow by 12 percent, which is better than average. It predicts that jobs for high school teachers will grow by 6 percent in the same time period. However, this prediction is for all teachers in all disciplines. It doesn't take into consideration the chronic shortage of high school math teachers, a situation that is likely to translate into more job opportunities for those who teach math.

Employment opportunities also look good for curriculum developers and postsecondary educators. According to the BLS, by 2022 job growth for curriculum developers is estimated to grow by 13 percent and by 19 percent for postsecondary educators.

Find Out More

Association of Mathematics Teacher Educators (AMTE)
website: http://amte.net

The AMTE is a large professional association of math educators. Members include college professors, K-12 math teachers, curriculum specialists, and graduate students. It provides job listings, information about graduate programs, conferences, publications, and news about math education.

Educators Rising

website: www.educatorsrising.org

Educators Rising is an organization for high school students interested in becoming teachers. It provides information about careers in teaching and scholarship opportunities.

Mathematical Association of America (MAA)

website: www.maa.org

The MAA is a professional society whose members include teachers, college professors, students, and mathematicians. It provides lots of information related to math and math careers, including resources for math educators.

National Council of Teachers of Mathematics (NCTM)

website: www.nctm.org

The NCTM offers career information, classroom resources, conferences, and publications. It also provides scholarships to college students interested in becoming math teachers.

Information Technology

A Few Facts

Number of Jobs
About 2 million

Salaries
$33,790 to
$140,460

**Educational
Requirements**
Minimum of a
bachelor's degree

Personal Qualities
Good analytical
and communication
skills; problem
solver; tech-savvy;
tenacious

Work Settings
Indoors in an office

Future Job Outlook
Job growth of 37
percent expected
by 2020, which is
much faster than
average

Information Technology Is All About Math

Lots of kids use their computers, tablets, and smartphones all the time. But some kids don't just *use* them; some kids spend hours tinkering with the devices and the software and learning the intricacies of interacting with the Internet. Some kids create their own apps or games; others follow or compete in hackathons with other tech-savvy folks. Welcome to the world of information technology (aka IT), which happens to be one of the hottest career fields around. IT is not just one type of job either; it's a multifaceted field. It's about software, data use and storage, and cybersecurity. It's about keeping computer systems, networks, and software running efficiently. It's about troubleshooting problems whenever they arise (and they do arise—all the time). It's about interfacing with all manner of devices, from smartphones to PCs. And the common denominator in all of this, believe it or not, is math.

No matter their title or job, IT professionals use mathematical thinking, analysis, and problem-solving skills. They use mathematical models and numerical calculations, too. As Jessie Caruso, a senior systems integrator, explains in an interview on the Mathematical Association of America website,

> My position entails meeting with customers from various sites, worldwide, collecting their system and software requirements, and then constructing the best, most efficient IT solution. This solution provides them with the network capability and system functionality they need to complete their daily, vital jobs. . . . My mathematical background has taught me how to approach these challenges in a logical fashion. I use my learned problem solving skills to respond, adapt and successfully address any problems or glitches that arise.

You Could Be a Systems Analyst

If an IT career interests you, you have lots of occupations to choose from. Some popular IT careers include IT manager, tech support specialist, cloud architect, database administrator, and web developer, among others. All IT careers are high-growth, in-demand occupations. In fact, the Bureau of Labor Statistics (BLS) predicts that by 2020 there will be more than 4.2 million IT and computer science jobs in the United States. Systems analyst is one of these growing careers.

Systems analysts evaluate computer systems or networks to make sure they're actually doing the things a business or other entity needs them to do—and that these tasks are being carried out efficiently. Let's say, for instance, that an advertising firm has a computer system with graphic capabilities but that system is too slow, too old, or too difficult to use. A systems analyst would meet with the firm's art department to discuss the problem. A careful analysis would reveal where the problem lies and likely lead to a proposed solution (such as hardware and software upgrades). Analysis of the costs and benefits of the old system and

A Typical Day for a Network Administrator

"Every day is new. There is so much diversity in your days because of the different issues that come up. Most days I have to be the face of our department, and I have meetings all day long. I work a lot with Active Directory, our database of users. . . . I do reboots every once in a while, which is pretty basic. However you need to make sure that everybody is ready. It is very business-critical, and you need to be focused on what you are doing when you are working in the server environment."

Ben Kuehn, quoted in "Interview with Ben Kuehn, Network Administrator," CareerColleges .com. www.careercolleges.com.

the upgrades would help management decide how to proceed. If a new system is approved, the systems analyst helps supervise its installation and configuration. They sometimes also write the computer programming code for the system's software programs to follow, or the coding may be done by another IT specialist known as a system programmer.

Network Administrator: A Hands-On Job

If you prefer a more hands-on job, you might consider another in-demand IT job: network administrator. Network administrators keep existing computer systems and networks running smoothly. A computer network is a group of computers, peripheral devices, and mobile equipment that communicates with a mainframe computer, known as a server, on which software and data are stored. If you like solving problems and working with your hands, this may be the occupation for you.

Network administrators are responsible for managing the company's server. This includes installing and configuring hardware and software, doing upgrades and repairs, and maintaining the network on a day-to-day basis. If problems arise, either on the network or on an employee's individual workstation, the network administrator is the wizard who solves them. In an interview on the website Career Colleges, Wisconsin network administrator Ben Kuehn calls such work "very high-stress problem solving. You have to think on your feet and act quickly when the servers are down and a company is losing money."

Cybersecurity Superheroes

One group of IT professionals is rapidly becoming the superheroes of cyberspace. They may not have Superman's talents to leap over tall buildings at a single bound, but they do work tirelessly to avert cybercrimes of all sorts. Cybersecurity analysts (aka information security analysts) are an up-and-coming career in an already hot field. These IT experts monitor websites and computer networks to protect sensitive data from cyberthieves. If they find a weakness, they are charged with fixing it. In addition, cybersecurity analysts establish information security policies, perform risk assessment tests, and encrypt sensitive data. The last is the process of encoding data using mathematical algorithms so that only authorized personnel have access.

This occupation is one of the fastest growing in the IT field. In fact, employers report that there are often as many as one hundred cybersecurity job openings for each qualified candidate. And the field is expected to keep expanding. The BLS predicts it will grow by 37 percent through 2022, which is more than three times the average for all careers. In an article on BankInfoSecurity.com, Rainer Steinwandt, the associate director and coeditor of the *Journal of Mathematical Cryptology*, agrees: "Data encryption and security is a huge and growing field today. New companies pop up daily that need to have data encrypted; they do that . . . using mathematics."

How Much Education Do You Need?

Educational requirements for IT careers vary. Occupations like web developers, help desk specialists, and tech support specialists require a minimum of an associate's degree. Most other IT careers require a bachelor's degree in math, computer science, or information technology. Postsecondary coursework will include classes in math and business as well as courses specific to IT, such as classes in communication networks, systems analysis, computer interfaces, and web design.

To help you prepare for an IT career, you should take advanced math and computer science classes in high school. Classes that improve your communication skills, such as speech and language arts, are also helpful.

Do You Need Any Certificates or Licenses?

IT specialists are not required to have any certificates or licenses, but earning different certifications can help you advance in your career. For example, candidates can become certified computer professionals in network administration, information security, computer hardware, cloud computing, or programming. In a 2014 article on the TechRepublic website, Kenton Scearce, the regional director of career services at East Coast Polytechnic Institute, explained that "IT certifications can net candidates an additional 5–15 percent increase in salary (from various reports and data). They also make you much more marketable as a candidate, since certification standards are constantly updated to keep current with the latest in technology trends."

Many organizations, including software firms like Microsoft, offer certification programs. Certification requirements vary by the career field, but most require individuals to have an associate's or a bachelor's degree and successfully complete a certification exam.

Exploring IT Careers

There are lots of ways to learn about and prepare for an IT career. One of the best ways is to participate in an IT internship while in college. Interns get to work with experienced IT professionals who will help them grow their IT skills. Many IT

Math Is a Common Language

"I've found that my math background is the most valuable asset that I have. My math skills, in general, help me to abstract concepts to better design software and solve problems. I am able to talk to a wide range of customers from different fields because of the common language of math. More importantly, I've found that my experience with numerical algorithms and software is not common, especially in the software industry. I've been able to get jobs easily and to always work on interesting problems."

Mary Beth Hribar, "Profiles of Professional Mathematicians and Computational Scientists," Society for Industrial and Applied Mathematics, 2015. www.siam.org.

internships are paid positions that offer college credit. And don't be surprised if the company you intern with offers you full-time employment upon your graduation. As Kyle Ewing, an intern supervisor at Google, comments in an article on the Fast Company website, "We look at our intern program as the best source of full-time talent, and it is our hope that every intern who performs well will be able to find a full-time opportunity at Google." Internships include summer and year-round programs and are offered by all types of businesses, governmental agencies, and other organizations.

Do You Have What It Takes to Succeed in IT?

To succeed in an IT career, you should have strong computer, analytical, and problem-solving skills. Good communication skills are also vital. IT professionals work in almost every industry all over the world. They often have to explain technical processes in easy-to-understand terms to clients, coworkers, and others who are not IT experts. They also have to write reports and proposals, making the ability to speak and write clearly essential.

IT professionals work with many different people. Being able to get along well with others and function as part of a team is a real plus. Flexibility, persistence, and creativity is essential. Not every IT challenge can be solved easily. IT specialists often face setbacks in their work. They need to be flexible enough to look for other solutions, creative in coming up with different answers, and unwilling to give up until the problem is solved.

Flexibility is also important when it comes to the hours this career field requires. Most IT professionals work a traditional forty-hour workweek. But some, like network administrators, are on-call day and night to address network problems as they occur. On Career Colleges, network administrator Kuehn says, "Technically I work 6:30 a.m. to 3:30 p.m., but most days I work to about 6 p.m. I also am on call every third week on off-hours, and every fifth weekend I have server reboots on Sundays at 4 a.m."

Earnings and Advancement

Wages vary depending on the particular job. In general, IT professionals are well paid. For example, in May 2014 the BLS reported the following mean annual salaries for these IT careers: network administrators, $79,770; systems analysts, $87,320; information security analysts, $91,600; and web developers, $68,670. It also reported that the lowest-paid 10 percent of IT professionals earn less than $33,790, and the highest-paid 10 percent earn more than $140,460.

In most cases, IT professionals also receive employee benefits such as health insurance, retirement benefits, and paid vacation and sick days. And because there is such a big demand for IT workers, many firms offer other perks to lure employees and keep them happy. These extras often include free lunch and snacks, on-site haircuts and massages, and social events.

Successful, experienced IT professionals can advance to managerial positions in which they oversee an entire IT department. In addition, they may go on to start their own IT consulting firms.

What About the Future?

The future outlook for IT careers is exceptionally bright. By 2022 all IT careers are predicted to grow faster than average, with many expected to grow two to three times faster than average. Plus, with new innovations in technology, new IT careers keep popping up. So, if you decide to pursue an IT career, chances are employers will be quite interested in hiring you.

Find Out More

Association of Information Technology Professionals (AITP)
website: www.aitp.org

The AITP seeks to advance IT professions and education. It has student chapters at colleges and universities, and it provides information about careers, IT education, and job postings.

Institute for the Certification of Computing Professionals (ICCP)
website: www.iccp.org

The ICCP provides information about certification, study materials, and certification tests for a variety of IT professions.

Network Professional Association (NPA)
website: www.npa.org

In addition to being an association of networking professionals, the NPA is also a resource for students hoping to pursue a networking career. It offers information about certifications, various publications, educational opportunities, tips on finding a job, and job postings.

Women in Technology (WIT)
website: www.womenintechnology.org

WIT is an organization that supports and promotes careers for women in technology. It offers special Girls in Technology programs to introduce young women to technology careers. It also provides job postings, networking opportunities, and career information.

Market Research Analyst

A Few Facts

Number of Jobs
As of 2014, about 468,160

Salaries
As of May 2014, the mean annual salary was $68,700

Educational Requirements
Minimum of a bachelor's degree

Personal Qualities
Analytical; methodical; detail oriented; good communication skills

Work Settings
Indoors in an office

Future Job Outlook
Job growth of 32 percent by 2022, making it one of the fastest-growing careers

What Do Market Research Analysts Do?

Burger King thought it had a real moneymaker when it introduced Satisfries, a supposedly healthier alternative to regular fries. McDonald's thought the same about its Mighty Wings. Both products flopped. Mistakes like these are embarrassing and costly, and no company wants to have this sort of thing happen. For that reason, many companies hire market research analysts. Market research analysts are business professionals who collect and analyze all sorts of data to determine what drives consumers to make the choices that they do. Their work has a big influence on what sorts of products and services businesses develop, how products are priced, and how and where products are marketed and sold. As marketing executive Jennifer Hirt-Marchand explains on an August 15, 2015, blog post on Market Research.com, "Doing business without market research is like sailing without a compass. . . . Market research helps to reduce risk, identify options, increase confidence, and provide an objective perspective necessary to direct a growing enterprise."

Market Researchers Answer Million-Dollar Questions

"Marketing research has endless questions for curious minds, the mental challenge itself is great fun. Why do people choose Coke over Pepsi? How do you successfully launch a new product and stun everyone? Is it worthwhile to purchase a billboard in New York's Time Square for promotion? Many questions that are raised and answered in marketing research are million dollar questions which could be heard in executive board meetings or seen in Wall Street journals. The answers to these questions could impact a public company's annual report, or even the entire brand's legacy."

Min Nie, "Why I Love MR," Wisconsin School of Business, March 16, 2014. http://bus .wisc.edu.

Market researchers are responsible for collecting and sifting through mounds of numerical data concerning consumer preferences, needs, and buying habits. They also collect data regarding competitors' products, and market conditions and trends. Then, using specialized statistical analysis software, they analyze the data in order to determine a wide range of things. For instance, their analysis helps companies to pinpoint who uses a particular product, what features consumers want in a specific product, and what they'll pay for a specific product. It also helps establish how effective an advertising campaign is, how sales vary by geographic regions or times of the year, and how the packaging of a product affects sales. In short, by analyzing data related to past sales, market research analysts are able to make predictions about future sales.

Once their analysis is complete, the next task is preparing statistical and written reports, spreadsheets, graphs, and tables detailing the findings, which are presented to management. Based on this work, companies might develop new products, redesign existing ones, or plan new marketing and advertising campaigns, among other things. As Stephen Griffiths comments in a blog post on the Wisconsin School of Business website, "Knowing that my efforts could shape the future of a company or product category is what keeps me in this field."

Where Does Math Fit In?

This is a career that uses math on a daily basis. If you become a market research analyst, you'll rely on the analytical skills that a strong math background imparts to understand, break down, and interpret large amounts of data. Indeed, your analytical skills, combined with your ability to identify patterns, will help you detect market patterns and problem areas.

Problem-solving skills are also crucial. Market research analysts spend a lot of time figuring out why things happen: why sales on one product are climbing while sales on a comparable product are falling; why sales are better in one geographic location than another; or why seasonal sales slumps occur. Identifying the *why* behind a problem is only one part of what market research analysts do; the next step is coming up with a logical solution. Moreover, although they use specialized statistical software programs in their work, their math skills must be super sharp. It would be almost impossible to understand what the software is doing, and whether the results are good, without an understanding of statistics and the different formulas and equations the software uses.

Market research analysts also use their math skills in reporting their findings, particularly in constructing and explaining graphs, statistical reports, and spreadsheets. As market research manager Jenny Dickson explains in an article on the *Guardian* website, "A reasonable level of numeracy [mathematical ability] and an analytical mind are necessary for breaking down the research objective and interpreting data."

How Do You Become a Market Research Analyst?

Employers want market research analysts to have a minimum of a bachelor's degree in market research or a related field, such as statistics or math. Having a master's degree, however, helps individuals advance in the field. To prepare for this career, high school students should take as many math classes as they can; economics also offers useful preparation for this career. Language arts and speech classes are also important. Market research analysts give oral and written reports of their findings. Language arts and speech classes will give you the skills and confidence to do so in a clear, effective manner.

College coursework is likely to include classes in economics, business administration, marketing, computer science, math, statistics, and data analysis. Psychology classes are also useful. Understanding what makes people tick helps market research analysts predict consumers' buying habits.

Preparing for This Career

If market research sounds like the career you've been searching for but you want to learn more, a good way to do so is by becoming a member of the Distributive Education Clubs of America (DECA), an association that introduces high school students to marketing careers. DECA members get to attend career development, networking, and leadership training events. In addition, DECA sponsors over $300,000 in college scholarships.

Participating in a college internship is another great way to learn about this career while gaining relevant work experience under the supervision of marketing professionals. Interns learn by doing. They're involved in a wide range of market research activities, such as gathering and interpreting consumer feedback, analyzing sales data, and preparing reports, among other projects. Plus, it's not unusual for internship positions to serve as stepping stones to full-time employment. College counselors can help locate suitable internships. Likewise, internship opportunities are found on the Internet as well.

Do You Have the Right Skills?

Market research is all about numbers, but it's not *only* about numbers. It's also about people and human behavior. So, besides

After gathering relevant data, a market research analyst develops a graph that will help him evaluate the direction his company wishes to go. Many companies highly value this type of research.

having a solid background in math, a knack for solving problems, and a foundation in economics, market research analysts need to have a healthy interest in people and the forces that motivate them. As market research analyst Min Nie noted in a March 2015 blog post on the Wisconsin School of Business website, "In my opinion, marketing research is truly made for those with curious minds who enjoy challenges. . . . A good marketing researcher should have decent knowledge in economics, psychology, and history apart from the quant/qual [quantitative and qualitative data analysis skills]. It takes so much to be a good detective and to discover the truth in consumer insights."

The ability to communicate clearly orally and in writing is essential, too. Market research analysts must be able to present their findings and recommendations in a way that clients, management, and other marketing professionals can understand. In addition, they should be able to work well with others. Market research analysts interact with advertising professionals, social media specialists, product developers, and field interviewers, among others. At the same time, they do a lot of independent work, such as analyzing data and preparing reports and graphs. Therefore, they also need to be comfortable working on their own.

What Will the Workplace Be Like?

Almost every industry depends on data analysis to understand and predict consumer buying trends. Market research analysts can choose to work in almost any industry that interests them—be it fashion, food, or music, to name a few. They may work for a private business, an educational institute, a health care organization, or a government agency. In addition, they may find employment with marketing, advertising, or consulting firms that do market research for many clients.

No matter the employer, the typical market research analyst works indoors in a comfortable office environment seated in front of a computer for large chunks of time. Analysts put in a traditional forty-hour workweek during traditional business hours. However, they may be required to work overtime to meet tight deadlines. At such times, this can be a fast-paced, high-pressure job.

Earnings and Advancement Opportunities

Market research analysts earn a comfortable income. In May 2014 the Bureau of Labor Statistics (BLS) reported that the median annual salary for market research analysts was $68,700. According to the BLS, average wages ranged from about $33,460 to about $116,740. Salaries vary depending on the analyst's years of experience and education level, the type of employer, and the geographic location of the job. The BLS also reported that California, Washington, Colorado, and Delaware have the highest mean salaries for this profession, and the following metropolitan areas have the highest mean annual salaries: San Jose, California, $108,680; San Francisco, $90,100; Seattle, $84,110; Oakland, California, $82,990; and Denver, $82,240.

In addition to a base salary, in most cases market research analysts receive employee benefits that include health insurance, retirement benefits, and paid vacation and sick days. Moreover, with successful work experience, analysts have lots of opportunities for advancement. Prime candidates for management positions show an understanding of data and consumer behavior, have knowledge of different markets and marketing trends, and have the ability to work both independently and with a variety of people. In fact, many top business executives have this type of marketing background.

A Fast-Growing Future

This is one of the fastest-growing careers in the United States. The BLS predicts that by 2022 employment opportunities for market research analysts will grow by 32 percent, which is about three times the average for all careers. This translates to about 131,500 new jobs in addition to current positions. The reason behind this growth is that in recent years businesses have become more and more aware of the value of analyzing data in giving

The Right Skills

"I spend a lot of time performing precise data analysis, hence being detail-oriented is critical. Patience and persistence are also necessary . . . because I need to devote long hours to independent study and problem solving. At the same time, I must work well with others as market researchers sometimes oversee the interviewing of individuals. Communication skills are important, too, because the wording of surveys is critical, and researchers must be able to present their findings both orally and in writing. A multitasking skill is essential for this job since I am running several projects at the same time."

Caroline Mojica, "Responsibilities as a Market Research Executive," A Day in the Life of a Market Researcher (blog), January 20, 2011. http://my-marketresearch-experience.blog spot.com.

them a competitive edge. This has created an increased need for market research analysts. Matt Ferguson, the chief executive of CareerBuilder and the coauthor of *The Talent Equation*, understands the importance of this career. In a January 14, 2014, article on the Economic Modeling Specialists International website, Ferguson explained that "individuals who can leverage data to zero in on new markets for growth will continue to be in demand."

Find Out More

American Marketing Association (AMA)
website: www.ama.org

The AMA is an association made up of marketing professionals and business educators. It provides information about marketing careers, job postings, publications, and webcasts.

Council of American Survey Research Organizations (CASRO)
website: www.casro.org

CASRO is an organization that represents the market research industry. It provides information about a career in market research, university programs in market research, job postings, and industry news. It also gives tips on preparing a résumé.

Distributive Education Clubs of America (DECA)
website: www.deca.org

DECA is an organization that helps high school and college students learn about marketing careers. Members can participate in volunteer work, attend workshops, enter competitions, and win scholarships.

Marketing Research Association
website: www.marketingresearch.org

This is a professional organization for market research specialists. It offers information about the profession and certification and also provides job listings.

Personal Finance

It's All About Money

Many people hate thinking about money, the future, savings and retirement, credit and debt, and other financial issues. So, they hire someone to think about it for them, or at least to help them sort through seemingly endless options and decisions. For this type of help, they turn to personal finance professionals. Personal finance is a broad occupational field that includes accountants, financial advisers, bankers, insurance agents, and wealth managers. Professionals in all of these occupations help people deal with their finances. One such individual is Theodore Sarenski, a certified public accountant (CPA) in Syracuse, New York. In an interview on the American Institute of Certified Public Accountants (AICPA) website, Sarenski comments, "I love the sincere appreciation you get from clients when you've helped make their financial life clearer for them and better in the future."

Personal finance professionals don't all do the same thing. For instance, insurance agents concentrate on helping people meet their insurance needs, and bankers assist bank customers manage the assets they have in the bank. Wealth managers concentrate on helping wealthy people handle multiple aspects of their personal finances, including investments, family businesses, estate and retirement planning, insurance requirements, and managing risk. In an article on the Bloomberg Business website, New York wealth manager Kevin Peters explains, "What my group does is specialize in complex family wealth—generational business, investing, estate planning."

The Role of Financial Advisers

Getting financial advice isn't just for the wealthy. Financial advisers (aka financial planners) work with middle- and upper-income people who need help making financial decisions. Whether it's planning for retirement, accumulating enough money to purchase a house, or paying college tuition, financial advisers devise plans that instruct people on the best ways to meet their financial goals.

In order to come up with a plan, financial advisers meet with clients to discuss their overall financial picture and their financial goals. Then, using their math skills and specialized software, they come up with a financial plan, which includes graphs and charts, detailing how the clients can reach their goals through specific investment strategies. They take into consideration a client's current income and expenses, financial goals, and risk tolerance, among other information.

It's All About People

"Some people think my job is all about numbers, money and taxes. They assume it's boring. I let them know it's really about people, and nothing could be better. . . . They're so interesting. Everyone has a story; who they are, what they do, where they come from and where they want to go."

Jean-Luc Bourdon, "Jean-Luc Bourdon, Financial Advisor," American Institute of Certified Public Accountants, 2015. www.startheregoplaces.com.

If the client approves of the plan, financial advisers invest the client's money and monitor the account, making adjustments as needed to improve the account's performance or to accommodate changes in the client's goals. They touch base with clients frequently. In fact, many financial advisers develop decades-long relationships with their clients. Patrick Canion, an Australian financial planner, notes in an article on the Financial Planet website, "I savor sitting down with clients, pausing to review their achievements over the years and congratulating them on what they have done."

Accountants Do Many Things

Accounting is another common finance career. Accountants prepare and analyze financial documents and keep records of financial transactions for individuals and businesses. There are many different types of accounting specialties, including forensic accounting, which investigates financial fraud, and private or management accounting, which deals with financial matters for businesses. Personal finance professionals typically are CPAs. An important part of a CPA's work is helping clients with tax issues. This involves reviewing the client's financial records, computing their taxes, and preparing their tax returns. And, if a client has tax problems or is audited by state or federal tax agencies, an accountant's job is to represent his or her client and help provide solutions.

CPAs also serve as financial advisers. In fact, some CPAs hold the title of CPA/PFS (personal financial specialist). Having this dual title is quite prestigious. In this capacity, CPAs advise their clients on diverse financial decisions that affect every part of their lives, including investments, tax matters, business matters, and estate planning, just to name a few areas. Mitchell Freedman is the president of a California accounting firm in which he serves as accountant and financial adviser to clients in the entertainment industry. In an interview on the AICPA website, he describes his job: "One day I could be helping with the negotiation of the terms of a director's contract for work, and another I could be flying to Utah to help another client evaluate a piece of real estate he's considering purchasing."

A financial adviser discusses earnings, tax, and investment information to help his clients meet their financial goals. Financial advisers often develop charts and graphs to illustrate various options.

Getting an Education

If you want to pursue a career in personal finance, you'll need a bachelor's degree. If your goal is to become a CPA, you should major in accounting. Popular majors for other personal finance careers include accounting, finance, business administration, mathematics, and economics. Coursework includes required liberal arts classes and courses specific to your major, such as tax law, investment analysis, and business writing. Psychology courses are good electives because they help you understand human behavior, which prepares you for dealing with clients. Computer science classes are also important, especially those that provide instruction in using financial software.

You should take as many business classes as possible in high school to prepare for postsecondary classes. What's more, high school business classes give you a chance to sample subjects like accounting and finance and see if you like them. As CPA Robyn Fuller explained in an August 12, 2014, article on the Black Enterprise website, "My interest in accounting came from a high school accounting class in the eleventh grade. Even as a young girl, I would play with calculators and I always wanted to add up money. Accounting was always something I naturally gravitated to." Classes in speech and language arts are also important. They help improve communication skills, which CPAs use on the job.

What About Certification and Licenses?

In addition to earning a bachelor's degree, accountants and financial planners should be licensed and/or certified. CPAs are licensed by their state's Board of Accountancy. Depending on the state, certification requires a bachelor's degree, at least two years of accounting work experience, and successful completion of a four-part qualifying exam. To become a certified financial adviser (CFA), candidates are required to have a bachelor's degree, at least three years of relevant work experience, pass an exam, and agree to follow a code of ethics.

Personal finance professionals can earn other licenses and certificates related to their careers. For instance, CPAs can earn a PFS credential by completing seventy-five hours of relevant education, having two years of financial planning work experience, and successfully completing an exam. Additional certificates and licenses are not required by law. However, they are prestigious and help individuals advance in their careers.

Exploring and Preparing

If you want to learn more about a career as a CPA or a financial adviser, a good way to do so is by job shadowing a professional through a typical workday. Another good way to learn more about accounting and get experience working with numbers is by serving as a treasurer of a club or team.

Doing a college internship with an accounting or financial planning firm is another good way to explore this field. Interns get a chance to gain practical experience under the mentorship of experienced professionals. And they make valuable connections that often help them gain full-time employment in the future. To sweeten the deal, these fields offer many paid internships.

What It Takes to Work in Personal Finance

CPAs and financial advisers work with numbers and analyze facts and figures on a daily basis. Therefore, math skills are vital to these careers. But math skills alone do not guarantee success. Personal finance careers are service oriented and require good interpersonal skills. To succeed in this field, you should enjoy interacting with others and be able to handle all types of people with tact and grace. Establishing a good rapport with clients is crucial. Clients trust CPAs and financial advisers with their life savings. Therefore, high ethical standards, integrity, and confidentiality are essential character traits for personal finance professionals.

Having good communication skills is also necessary. Being able to ask and answer questions concerning your client's finances in layman's terms is especially useful. In an interview on the AICPA website, Louisiana CPA Magen Smith cautions, "It's important to be able to explain what information you need from people in a way that they can understand. Often, they don't know our terminology or fully understand what we do, so we need to bridge that gap."

Work Environment

Personal finance professionals work in a comfortable office environment. They spend a lot of time seated in front of a computer. Employers vary. CPAs usually work for accounting firms, but they may be self-employed as well. Most financial advisers are employed by financial planning firms. They also work for banks, brokerage firms, and mutual fund and insurance companies.

Most CPAs and financial planners work a traditional forty-hour workweek. However, it is common for financial advisers to meet with clients in the evening or on weekends, and CPAs often work long hours during tax season.

An All-Around Career

"Each and every day is different. And each day is interesting and challenging. If you want the opportunity to earn lots of money and have a stimulating, challenging career, becoming a CPA is the way to go."

Elizabeth Shwiff, "Elizabeth Shwiff, Senior Founding Partner," American Institute of Certified Public Accountants, 2015. www.startheregoplaces.com.

Good Pay and Opportunities for Advancement

Personal finance professionals are paid well and have opportunities for advancement. According to the Bureau of Labor Statistics (BLS), as of 2014 accountants earned between $40,850 and $115,950, with a mean annual salary of $73,670.

Earnings for financial advisers are determined in a variety of ways. Some are paid a predetermined annual salary. Some earn a percent of the assets they manage; this can be quite lucrative for financial advisers with lots of clients. Some charge clients an hourly fee for their services, and others receive commissions for the financial products that they sell. Often, these professionals' income is based on a combination of these methods. In any case, the BLS reports a mean annual salary of $108,090 for financial advisers, with salaries ranging from about $35,500 to $139,350. Besides wages, CPAs and financial advisers often receive employee benefits that include health insurance, retirement benefits, and paid vacation and sick days.

Gifted accountants and financial planners have lots of chances to advance in their careers. As financial planners expand their client base, their income grows. With successful work experience, many go into business for themselves, as do some accountants. CPAs can also advance to managerial positions and eventually become partners in large firms. Moreover, CPA skills also are in demand in the world of big business. In fact, many chief financial officers at large corporations are CPAs.

What About the Future?

Future employment opportunities look good for personal finance professionals. The BLS predicts that by 2022 jobs for accountants will grow by 13 percent and by 27 percent for financial planners. In both cases, this is better than average.

Find Out More

AccountingMajors.com
website: www.accountingmajors.com

This website serves as a resource for accounting majors and students interested in an accounting career. It provides information about scholarships, internships, and links to related sites.

American Institute of Certified Public Accountants (AICPA)
website: www.aicpa.org

The AICPA represents the accounting profession. It provides information about becoming a CPA, different accounting careers, certifying exams, and salary data as well as interviews with professionals. Student membership is available.

Financial Planning Association (FPA)
website: www.fpanet.org

The FPA is a professional organization of certified financial advisers; it includes membership options for students. It provides information about the career and promotes financial education for youth.

Learn How to Become
website: www.learnhowtobecome.org

This website provides information about many different careers. Its page on financial advisers gives information about the career and the steps needed to become a financial adviser. It includes an interview with a financial adviser and salary information.

Statistician

A Few Facts

Number of Jobs
As of 2014, about 26,970

Salaries
As of 2014, the mean annual salary was $84,010

Educational Requirements
Minimum of a master's degree

Personal Qualitites
Good problem-solving skills; ability to work well with others; detail oriented; logical

Work Setting
Indoors in an office

Future Job Outlook
Job growth of 27 percent is expected by 2022, which is much faster than average

Using Statistics to Change the World

There's no way around it: *statistician* just doesn't sound like a thrilling job. But if people really knew what statisticians do, they might think differently about this career. The fact is that statisticians work in medical research, agriculture, manufacturing, public policy, and even sports. Statisticians work with statistics, which is the science of learning through data. Statisticians use mathematics in combination with statistical software to gather and analyze numerical data in an effort to solve practical problems. Through their work, they make a difference in all sorts of fields.

The job of the statistician revolves around collecting, organizing, and interpreting data in order to solve a particular problem. This is more complex than it sounds. Before any data can be collected, statisticians must decide exactly what type of data is needed, the type and size of the sample or subjects to be studied, and the best method for getting the required data. (Common methods include polls, surveys, experiments, and medical trials.) Depending on the problem, statisticians design the data collection method or collaborate with other professionals, such as physicians and research scientists, to do so.

Once the data has been collected, the next step is organizing and interpreting it. If you're curious and like solving puzzles, here's where the real fun begins. Like detectives, statisticians look for patterns and trends in the data that relate to the problem. They use specialized statistical software, algorithms, and mathematical formulas in their analysis. And to ensure that the data is valid, they conduct statistical tests on it. When the analysis is done, statisticians present their findings in the form of oral presentations and written reports that include statistics, tables, and graphs.

Match Your Interests to Your Specialty

The problems statisticians work on cut across every sector of society and every industry. Statisticians can be generalists and tackle problems in many different areas, or they can specialize in a particular field or industry. This is good news for people with multiple passions who'd like to combine their love of math with their other interests. For example, if you're fascinated by health issues, you can become a biostatistician or biometrician. These statisticians are involved in medical research. On the Mathematical Association of America website, biostatistician Ellen Lentz discusses her job at a large pharmaceutical firm:

> Why would discovering a new medicine have anything to do with statistics? Well, in order to know whether the drug works, we have to test it. . . . Often the results are not black or white. One question is how many patients need to be tested before we know a drug is effective and safe. How do we know these results are not purely due to chance? These are all statistical questions. I help the clinicians find the best way to conduct an experiment to answer the most important questions to them. I calculate the number of subjects needed in each trial in order to make a conclusion with a given certainty on the effect of a new drug.

If you'd rather solve problems concerning animals, plants, insects, and food production, you can specialize in agricultural statistics. Or, if sports are your thing, you can become a sports statistician. Just like in the movie *Moneyball*, sports statisticians gather and analyze data concerning the performances of individual athletes and sports teams. As Keith Woolner, a sports statistician with the Cleveland Indians, explains in an interview on the American Statistical Association (ASA) website, "We help baseball operations put the best possible team on the field. In many cases, that involves developing statistical models to measure player value, forecast future performance, and answer questions about game strategy and tactics."

Those concerned with social issues can join the ranks of governmental statisticians. They're usually employed by government agencies and tackle problems that affect public policy and social programs. Their work ranges from organizing and analyzing census data to working on matters involving crime, ecology, and social justice, just to name a few. As Emily Poskett, a British governmental statistician, explains in *Plus* magazine, "For any country, measuring poverty, the growth of the economy, unemployment and other socio-economic factors are essential in deciding on and testing political policy."

Statisticians work in many other fields. They can be found in all areas of business and industry. Some, like theoretical

Research That Matters

"I have worked as a statistician for three federal government agencies, each committed to health and environmental research. In these professional settings, I have had great latitude in determining which problems to address and how the work should proceed. I have done research for problems arising from water and waste water evaluation and treatment as well as in many fields of animal testing. . . . Some of the most challenging work has recently arisen from animals exposed to several regimens of ozone at different exposure temperatures."

Jerry Highfill, "Career Profiles: Jerry Highfill," Mathematical Association of America, 2015. www.maa.org.

statisticians, are researchers who develop new statistical methods. Others concentrate on engineering, computer science, education, or manufacturing.

The Fastest-Growing STEM Major

Statisticians need lots of schooling. Although a bachelor's degree may be accepted for an entry-level statistician job, most employers prefer candidates who have a master's degree in statistics or math. This typically takes two years of education beyond a bachelor's degree or a total of six years of education beyond high school. Undergraduate- and graduate-level courses should appeal to the math lover in you. Typical classes include statistical methods, differential calculus, linear algebra, probability theory, and data science. Many students combine these classes with a minor in whatever field they hope to work in. Students also take computer science classes so that they can work with data and use statistical software effectively.

As a statistics major, you'll be riding a growing wave. As of 2015, statistics was the fastest-growing STEM (Science, Technology, Engineering, Math) degree in the United States. "The main

The Demand for Statisticians Is Growing

"We're entering an era of tremendous growth in the profession of statistics that is not unlike the growth of computing professionals in the 1960s and 1970s. At that time, software engineers and programmers were still relatively rare, but grew quickly and steadily as computing became something every large company needed to remain competitive. We're seeing a similar trajectory in statistics. Advances in computing, technology and Big Data continue to raise the demand for statisticians."

David R. Morganstein, quoted in "More Students Earning Statistics Degrees, but Not Enough to Meet Surging Demand for Statisticians," American Statistical Association, October 1, 2015. www.amstat.org.

driver is the job market," says Frederic P. Schoenberg, chair of the Statistics Department at the University of California, Los Angeles (UCLA). In an article on the ASA website, Schoenberg comments that UCLA's "graduates are getting excellent jobs in industry with a statistics degree. Businesses throughout the country are forming analytics groups and seeing the value of data analysis. They are, therefore, hiring statisticians at a high rate and that is fueling our majors."

To prepare for a statistics career, you should take college prep courses in high school, including as many science and math classes as possible. Likewise, classes that improve communication skills, such as English and speech, are also important because statisticians are responsible for both written and oral reports and presentations.

Preparing for This Career

One of the best ways to prepare for this career is by doing an internship while in college. Interns get to attack real problems under the guidance of experienced statisticians and professionals from other fields. They're involved in designing studies and in collecting, organizing, and analyzing data from ongoing research projects. Internships are available in almost every industry and include medical research facilities, college athletic associations, insurance companies, sports teams, computer tech companies, and government agencies. To help students find internships, every December the ASA posts a list of upcoming summer internships on its website. College statistics and math departments can also help match students with internship opportunities. In many cases, students can earn college credit for participating in an internship. And, if all goes well, the employer may offer the intern a full-time job upon graduation.

Do You Have the Skills a Statistician Needs?

Mathematics is the basis of statistics. Statisticians should enjoy working with numbers and have good problem-solving and critical-thinking skills. These abilities help them analyze data, identify the strengths and weaknesses of a study, draw conclusions, and come up with different approaches to working on a problem.

Statisticians should also be detail oriented. They work with mountains of data. If they don't pay careful attention, they can overlook patterns or data irregularities, which can compromise their findings. They also need to be knowledgeable about whatever field they're working in and have good technical skills since statisticians spend a lot of time working on a computer.

Good speaking and writing skills, too, are necessary. Statisticians don't just work with numbers, they also have to explain their work. They're expected to communicate their findings to clients and professionals from other fields in a way everyone can understand. This means they must be able to translate statistical jargon into layman's terms. As statistician Woolner explains, "If you can't explain what you've analyzed to someone who doesn't have the same statistical training, you'll have a hard time influencing the decisions they make."

In addition, statisticians must be able to work well with others. Statisticians often work in teams. They interact and collaborate with other statisticians and professionals from a variety of other fields, many of whom are experts in their discipline. To do the best job, they need to listen to and respect their collaborators' input and be willing to learn from them.

Employers, Pay, and Advancement

Statisticians work in every industry as well as in universities in research positions. About one-fifth are employed by the federal government. Statisticians work in comfortable office environments. Just how much they're paid depends on the industry they work in, their education and experience, and the geographic location of the job. According to the Bureau of Labor Statistics (BLS), in May 2014 the mean annual salary for a statistician was $84,010, with the lowest-paid 10 percent of statisticians earning less than $43,840 and the highest-paid 10 percent earning more than $129,830.

Most statisticians work a traditional forty-hour workweek and receive employee benefits such as health insurance, retirement benefits, and paid vacation and sick leave. With a master's degree and successful work experience, statisticians can advance to supervisory positions in which they oversee other statisticians and research teams.

A Hot Skill with a Big Future

Statistics is a red-hot career field, which the BLS estimates will grow by 27 percent by 2022. Hal Varian, Google's chief economist, calls it "the sexy job in the next ten years." In a January 2009 interview in the *McKinsey Quarterly*, Varian said, "People think I'm joking, but who would've guessed that computer engineers would've been the sexy job of the 1990s? The ability to take data—to be able to understand it, to process it, to extract value from it, to visualize it, to communicate it—that's going to be a hugely important skill in the next decades." So, if working with data is your dream job, there is definitely a need for you in the workaday world.

Find Out More

American Statistical Association (ASA)
www.amstat.org

The ASA is the world's largest association of statisticians. It offers lots of information about a career in statistics, including information about colleges that offer degrees in statistics.

Master's in Data Science
www.mastersindatascience.org

This website provides information about careers in data science, including statistician, and information about university programs in data science.

Mathematical Association of America (MAA)

website: www.maa.org

The MAA is a professional society that provides lots of information related to math and math careers, including information about a career as a statistician.

World of Statistics

www.worldofstatistics.org

This international organization is dedicated to promoting careers in statistics and educating the public on the importance of statistics. It has lots of information about careers in statistics.

INTERVIEW WITH A FINANCIAL ADVISER

Gregg Boone is a financial adviser with LPL Financial in Arlington, Texas. He has worked as a financial adviser for twenty years. He spoke with the author by phone about his career.

Q: Why did you become a financial adviser?

A: I wanted to help other people and it was a way of making a good income while helping others. It's a rare place where the customer benefits and you benefit, too, so everybody wins.

Q: Can you describe a typical workday?

A: That's a good question! The first thing I do when I come into the office in the morning is check my e-mails and phone messages. Then, I call all the clients who have left messages and e-mails. Next, I pull up the stock market and check what's going on; then I look at my plans for the day. Then, I make calls to clients. I probably spend half the day calling clients. I spend the rest of the day doing an analysis of the economy, the stock market, and investment choices. I also work on financial plans for my clients.

Q: What do you like most and least about your job?

A: What I like most is helping clients' financial portfolios grow, so that they can reach their life goals—so that they can retire and not worry about money, and so that they can send their kids to college. It's great to know that I help people to reach a point where they don't have to worry about money.

What I like least is when the stock market drops and clients call me in a panic, despite the financial education about the ups and downs of the stock market that I've given them.

Q: What personal qualities do you find valuable for this type of work?

A: You have to be able to understand how other people feel about their money and life goals. You have to be able to listen to and understand what they tell you, then probe with the right questions. Communication skills are a big key. You have to be able to explain complex issues in easy-to-understand terms the client will understand, and different people understand things in different ways. And, you have to truly care about your clients. People will read through you if you don't care.

Another quality is you have to be someone who doesn't quit, and there are times I've wanted to quit. When you get bad markets, when clients panic, you have to be tenacious. And it goes without saying that you have to be good in math. You don't have to be an engineer with trigonometry-level math, but you have to be good in math. The most important thing on this job is you have to have people skills. You need your math, but you have to have people skills to succeed.

Q: How do you use math on the job?

A: I use it to calculate financial returns using cost analysis and to figure out how much money clients need to reach their financial goals. I have a financial computing calculator and software programs that run the numbers, but you have to be careful. You have to know how the numbers work to know if you're getting good results from your programs. You have to understand where the calculations are coming from, otherwise it's garbage in and garbage out.

Q: What was your favorite subject in school?

A: History. That builds into my job because if you look at history in relation to major financial events, you can better understand the future. People who call me in a panic about the stock market haven't studied financial history. Ironically, the class I hated the most in college was a finance class where you had to manually do calculations like factors that there are calculators for. I majored in business marketing and took finance classes.

Q: Did you ever think of doing something else?

A: I thought very seriously about becoming a scientist. I also thought about being a psychologist. I didn't because I thought working with people with problems all the time might affect me negatively. But I truly do use psychology on my job and I'm glad I do what I do. I love my job. My clients are all nice, and savers are smart people.

Q: What advice do you have for students who might be interested in this career?

A: In high school, study psychology, take basic financial classes on how to budget money and other real-world aspects of finance. Public speaking classes are also useful. I don't speak to groups, but if you can speak well in public, you can speak well one-on-one. Also, to get a feel for what I do, look up a financial calculator online. Use it to see how much money you'll have if you save $400 a month for forty years at 8 percent interest. Or, try it with $40 a month.

Q: Do you have anything else to add?

A: There's definitely a need for financial planners. There are not enough young people coming into the business. It's good for me—less competition. But for the next generation there's not going to be enough financial advisers.

OTHER CAREERS IF YOU LIKE MATH

Accounting clerk
Air traffic controller
Astronaut
Astronomer
Auditor
Banker
Bookkeeper
Cashier
Chef
Chemist
Claims adjuster
Cloud architect
Construction manager
Cost estimator
Database administrator
Data miner
Demographer
Economist
Electrical engineer

Electrician
Financial analyst
Forensic analyst
Geologist
Hospital administrator
Industrial engineer
Insurance underwriter
Logistician
Mathematician
Mechanical engineer
Nurse
Operations research analyst
Pharmacist
Physician
Physicist
Real estate agent
Sales representative
Stockbroker
Surveyor

Editor's note: The online *Occupational Outlook Handbook* of the US Department of Labor's Bureau of Labor Statistics is an excellent source of information on jobs in hundreds of career fields, including many of those listed here. The *Occupational Outlook Handbook* may be accessed online at www.bls.gov/ooh.

INDEX

78

PICTURE CREDITS

ABOUT THE AUTHOR

Barbara Sheen is the author of ninety-one books for young people. She lives in New Mexico with her family. In her spare time she likes to swim, walk, garden, and cook.